HOW TO WRITE COPY THAT SELLS

The Copywriting Secrets to Help You Promote Your Products and Services.

Your Guide to Business Writing That Charms, Captivates and Sells.

The Guide to Copywriting Secrets for Businessmen, Entrepreneurs and Copywriters.

By

Vladimir Malyuga

Table of Contents

Part 1. HOW TO MAKE RESUME TO COPYWRITER...........3

Part 2. HOW TO WRITE TEXT "ABOUT COMPANY" 11

Part 3. RECEPTION OF COPYWRITING "PROBLEM + THE DESIRED DECISION" 15

Part 4. 18 METHODS of MURDER ADVERTISEMENT TEXT.. 19

Part 5. 99 MARKETING IDEAS FOR COPYWRITING........27

    99 marketing ideas that most direct related to the copywriting market...27

Part 6. COMMERCIAL SUGGESTION 39

    6.1. FORMULA OF WRITING OF HEADING 49

    6.2. OFFER...55

    6.3. DEADLINE 59

    6.4. CALL TO ACTION 65

Part 7. CONCLUSION 68

Part 1. HOW TO MAKE RESUME

TO COPYWRITER

Whether that it is a period such enigmatic, whether that simply came to a head. Lately I all more often get requests from customers to write about that, how to make an executive summary for copywriters. If it to look at the executive summary of copywriters, then it is possible to understand for 5 seconds, as far as an author, in general, understandsin the work. Because as there are such elements that need to be known. HR- the specialists of many companies at once decline a candidature without consideration if elementary errors are seen.

We will begin with the "sharpest":

1. Do not write the word "CV" in the header. Name and surname should be instead.

2. Place of study and place of work are indicated in reverse chronological order.

3. Attach a photo. And once again - attach a photo. Strict, business and current.

4. Send resumes in PDF format, because when you open a document in MS Word or other text editors, because of the internal settings, the layout of the text may fly off - and an incomprehensible text mess appears in front of the potential employer.

5. The optimal volume of the resume - 1-2 pages. Do not turn it into a brochure or, God forbid, into an e-book.

6. Use classic and clear subtitles of blocks of summary. Without epithets and metaphors.

7. Subheadings in bold. Use no more than 2 fonts.

8. Avoid underscores. Otherwise, they might think that you are using a link.

9. 100 times subtract the summary for errors.

10. If you use the print version of the resume - do not save on paper. Let it bedense and snow-white.

Few applicants follow these obvious recommendations.

And before you, is a classic of the genre without reference to the profession.

Therefore, first study the theoretical basis, and then proceed to the preparation of your resume.

And here is another critical point - forget about examples of resume copywriters, which are in the public domain.

The only exception is professional HR resources and sources.

The main sections of the summary.

If you follow the classical structure of the compilation of the summary, then it is customary to single out the following structural elements of the summary:

• **Title** - here, as you already understood, in the upper part of the document indicate the name and surname of the applicant.

• **Personal data** - date of birth, age, and marital status.

• **Contact details** - everything is standard and clear. I also recommend adding your profile links to social networks - this will help employers understand how exciting and educated you are. So stay tuned to what you post on social networks.

• **Goal** - the employer is interested in what you pursue personal and professional goal, working in his company. The goal must always be specific, feasible and contain specific deadlines for implementation.

• **Education** - here you talk about your education, as in a regular resume.

• **Work experience** - no need to describe your entire professional biography. The employer is interested in the last 3 jobs. Be sure to tell the employer what exactly you did in each position that you have worked in. And make sure that your activity in its functionality matches what you are looking for.

If you were doing the same work at different places - do not try to copy one-to-one - your task is to show your versatility and versatility.

• **Additional information** - in this part, you have the opportunity to justify further why your candidacy should be considered more closely. What could be here? See the "buns", which I separately discuss below.

• **Professional skills** - a very important point in which you are able to stand out. It's not just praisingyourself but think more what the employer wants to read. My personal recommendations: focus on results, meeting deadlines and requirements for each project, ability to work in a team, deep immersion in each project, attention to detail, work with non-standard solutions - they understood the direction of thought.

• **Personal qualities** - I never considered this a key section of the resume, but, nevertheless, you can paint: honesty, politeness, specifics, accuracy, attentiveness, good memory, decency. My personal recommendation is to include in this item some of your excellent professional skills.

• **Hobbies and hobbies** - be careful here, because many employers are able to form certain impressions about a candidate on the items filled. I recommend to show you your originality and connection with the profession. Talk about cool hobbies, for example - the history of retro cars, extreme sports, avant-garde cinema, collecting samples of old print advertising, studying the history of brands, professional and business literature.

Other things being equal, employers want applicants to indicate their desired salary. Just no one wants to spend time figuring out what can be specified in advance.

Similarly, you also help yourself to weed out appeals that are notoriously unattractive for wages.

"Selling" additional information

Now go to the "buns".

No matter how popular the classics are, the result is guaranteed by buns. In order for your resume to attract the attention of a potential employer, equip it with special "buns".

Their number depends on what you can boast of justifying their ambitions.

1. **Additional education** - according to the logic of following this item goes right after the block "Education". Here, it is advisable to show you which training, courses, seminars you attended - and try to ensure that these courses on your subject fit the proposed work.

 And, by the way, be sure to point out that you are studying the areas that directly affect copywriting - marketing, sales, competition, behavior psychology, etc.

2. **Achievements** - if you have something to tell - go for it. For example, victories in contests of copywriters, high results for clients.

3. **Customers** - if you have experience of working with well-known customers or personalities - do not be silent, this will give your professionalism additional arguments "plus".

4. **Content-activity** - yes, I can write that I am the author of the book. But no one forbids you to write, for example: " I am the author of 25 articles on the topic of copywriting, which are published in _____". And if you are still printed in magazines - my applause.

5. **Thematic knowledge**: in the "additional information" you can indicate the wealth of topics and areas of activity for which you prepared the texts.

6. **Genre diversity** - show that you write texts of various genres and objectives - texts for websites, articles, offers, press releases, texts for email-letters, texts for selling pages, texts for commercials, etc.

7. **Recommendations** - if you have recommendations from previous employers or clients, do not hide them, they can strengthen your resume.

8. **Expectations** - a very bold and important point, just show your expectations from a new job. The employer is always looking for people who want to develop and find realization for their potential.

9. **Additional skills** - the employer likes to hire employees combining several activities. Suppose if you have design skills, layout is only a HUGE PLUS.

10. **Portfolio** - never understood phrases in the summary "Portfolio on request". You are not a celebrity, and you do not have a rider yet. Therefore, keep it simple. Many resumes have no portfolio at all. This is a HUGE MISTAKE! And I'm not afraid to use the word "mistake." Attach a summary of your portfolio to your resume. A portfolio includes demonstration works that prove your talents in different genres of text and areas of activity.

Competently approach the style of presenting information.

An intelligent copywriter always works not only on the essence and meaning but also on the presentation. The text can affect both the conscious and the subconscious. The text of the summary is similar, so write:

1. Specifically, don't write "trained new employees in copywriting," but indicate "taught 4 employees new copywriting and was the curator for the first 4 months of work".

2. Focusing on the result - instead of "preparing business proposals for customers," write "with the help of the business proposals I compiled, the company attracted 75 new customers." Just write the truth, do not fool yourself, then it comes around.

3. Without "procedural layers" - forget about "responsible for execution", "was engaged in development", "took part in" - write more energetically "performed", "developed", "participated".

4. Without even a hint of negative - compare yourself, which looks preferable - "corrected errors of ineffective text materials" or "improved and finished de text materials".

5. It is clear - do not try to impress the employer with the help of learned words and professionalisms that he may not know. This is not the case where you need to be clever.

And do not forget to print a resume to evaluate how it looks on paper. Because many clients just print out resumes to coordinate the candidate for consideration.

You have to make sure that the resume is well read, and that you have chosen the optimal font size and design - both for the electronic and for the printed version.

Each resume must be unique!

Your resume should be 75% prepared before the need to use it.

Here I mean that if you submit a resume for a specific vacancy - do not rush to send it in the form in which it has already been prepared.

Carefully read the requirements and wishes expressed in a particular vacancy.

For example, very often an employer indicates what exactly the employee he is looking for will do — this is your food for thought. What can you add, replace, rephrase in your functionality at previous places of work?

If the employer requests any additional non-standard information - provide it.

It's just that so many of them sift out candidates (for inattentively reading requirements).

Successes with job searches. Believe in you and keep cams!

Part2. HOW TO WRITE TEXT

"ABOUT COMPANY"

The text "About the company" should be in each company. But the question lies elsewhere - how to write a text about a company that can form the desired image and dispel the last doubts?

Today, I want to share with you a selection of 32 wise thoughts about the intricacies of writing texts about the company.

Enough already fill the pages of their sites with narcissistic odes; begin to follow the path of serious authors.

Bragging and falsehood - the first step to the loss of not only new customers but also existing ones.

Read, think about, change thinking and improve the texts of their own, and not only their companies.

1. The "About Company" text is a type of text that should be present by default on a corporate website.

2. Business owners and copywriters have no idea what to write in the text "About the Company".

3. The text "About the Company" is the only text where you can safely and in all colors praise yourself. But you need to submit the facts so that the reader himself draws conclusions about the degree of your coolness.

4. On the page "About the company" in general, people do not get right away. As a rule, after reading the text on the main page or the text describing the product, service.

5. The main task of the text "About the Company" is to provide a comprehensive answer to the question: "Why should I trust you?".

6. The biggest mistake that occurs in the "About the Company" texts is the absence of the company name.

7. "We just opened up, we don't have much to write about our company ..." - "Question: why did you open then, if you have nothing to tell the reader?"

8. In the "About the Company" text, a potential client is looking for reasons for cooperation and specific information that can dispel existing doubts.

9. It's one thing to read a "dry" text, and quite another to watch a competent and professional video message from the first person of the company.

10. If each company, by definition, must be unique, then why do they have 80 percent identical texts?

11. Pay attention to the texts on the pages of your direct competitors. Your potential customers will also read them.

12. I can distinguish two main styles of writing texts "About the Company" - business and organizational.

13. Tell about what you are doing and for whom.

14. A leader must behave like a leader everywhere. Therefore, no advertising notes, screams and appeals in every paragraph.

15. The reader should see in your company something special that could interest him. Conclusion - look for differences.

16. Do not call the block with its advantages a banal expression "Our advantages".

17. Companies that really have something to be proud of can always tell about themselves in pleasant figures.

18. If the site does not have a separate "About Services" page, then you can tell about them on the "About the Company" page.

19. For the consumer, you must become a new company not only by its "birth certificate", but also by its format.

20. A bold option for positioning is to voice yourself No.1 in something. Think of what. The narrower the niche, the greater the chance of becoming No.1 there.

21. We are not going to talk about a "dynamic growing company" and about gutta-percha logistics.

22. By and large, people do not need your goods and services, but the result that they want to achieve.

23. The only bump, about which copywriters and resource owners stumble with enviable regularity, is the veracity of the benefits listed in the "About the Company" text. If you write "we will deliver the goods within 24 hours", and in fact, your transport department works with a delay of a week, then there is no need to talk about success and trust.

24. The mission for the company is that the oath for the soldier and the "Hippocratic Oath" for the doctor.

25. The case is presented in a short format on the principle of "what was - what became".

26. Think about how to prove that it is beneficial for the client to work with you, and not just describe what others are doing.

27. If you have specific achievements (certificates, awards), then do not be shy. Show them to your customers.

28. The text "About the Company" is the most logical and effective place for social proofs of the effectiveness of an enterprise.

29. Do not brag, for "to boast is to say to others without courtesy: I am better than you."

30. Tell us about your plans for the future - show that you are not going to stop at what you have achieved, that you are looking for ways to develop and improve.

31. One common mistake in the texts of "About the Company" - they end without a call to action.

32. There is no single proven scenario for the text "About the Company", which will work in any field of activity.

Part 3. RECEPTION OF COPYWRITING "PROBLEM + THE DESIRED DECISION"

I want to share with you the reception of copywriting from my personal practice. I will tell you about a clever trick. Just show you how simple solutions can solve complex problems.

This technique is not the fruit of fantasy, but the result of practice.

That is, he was already working. Worked well and still does not give up their positions. Therefore, make yourself comfortable, turn on your rationality and carefully read everything I have written.

I will be brief, but accurate.

Persuasion tactics "Pain ... More Pain ..." - do not fall into euphoria

If you actively follow the literature of the topic of copywriting and specialized training, you have heard about such a formula as "Pain ... More Pain ..."

According to this formula, "pressing" a client's problem contributes to influencing his desire to get rid of it as soon as possible. Lightly pressed, then slightly strengthened and hit the target.

Example: Tired of having a constantly stuffy nose? And you do not feel much excitement from stuffing it with some kind of advertised drops? Which is enough for 2 hours.

Moreover, you are like a drug addict who, without these drops, does not represent a normal existence at all.

Good? Yes, very good.

With emotion, a few necessary words for the effect. The attention of the target audience should attract. But if you can do even better, why not?

When you connect a strong impact on some serious desire or dream, you also hit the target.

And you do it more gently and beautifully, rather than when "posing the problem" in the style of "Pain ... More Pain ...".

Example:

Do you want your nose to breathe clean air again without any obstacles? And no more drops. No dependency. Never.

Good? I like it too especially because it is very brief and apt.

But you can always make it even cooler. And here we come to the most important thing ... Ladies and gentlemen, problem + desired solution

See, there is a problem that the client wants to get rid of. At this stage, he, in principle, does not sit with folded arms.

He looks for solutions and tries different methods. But ... By posing a problem or indicating a desire in advertising, he is already full.

Now it is used everywhere. Like, aptly, but not completely.

The overwhelming majority of advertising messages are compiled as if for a carbon copy. Only the names of companies, products, prices, discount sizes, and other parameters change.

And the thing is that the client has his own idea of the ideal solution to his problem. But he does not know whether it exists. Therefore, looking for...

We voice the problem and suggest a solution that the client himself dreams of. "Here it is! There is! Just what I was looking for! "

Do you think this is a good emotion for sales? Sorry for the rhetorical question, could not resist.

How does the "Problem + Desired Solution" technique work?

And, of course, need an example.

Immediately I recall the good old formula headline "How to lose weight, enjoying five sweet dishes?".

True, not all heard about it. In this image, you can prepare different options:

• "How to get rid of hemorrhoids without surgery?"

• "How can a bachelor enjoy culinary delights without touching the stove?"

• "How to turn a failure product into a best-selling product without investing a penny in it?"

And you can go even further ... Suggest a way that in the eyes of the reader looks even cooler than his own perfect solution.

This is the result of dense and detailed work with the target audience.

Ideally, the "Problem + Desired Solution" technique works well for creating the desired first impression effect.

That is - the title and introductory part.

Part 4. 18 METHODS OF MURDER

ADVERTISEMENT TEXT

Now I wanted us to remember the fundamental truths from the classic copywriting.

Sometimes, the problem of low conversion or poor efficiency lies precisely in these truths.

At a time when we are trying to invent something revolutionary, then we do not pay attention to things that flow smoothly in front of us.

And this loss gradually destroys the effectiveness of our advertising texts.

We often say that someone gives us primitive advice, but we ourselves do not notice how we do not use them at all.

Whether because of pride, or because of inattention, or because of frank stupidity. We are tired of following the classic rules, calling them "trivial."

And, nevertheless, everything new is a well-forgotten classic. And sometimes a very well forgotten classic ...

Therefore, I want us to now together with you once and for all put together the main classical postulates when writing advertising texts.

I chose the following format - you will be offered a list of the most brutal ways to kill advertising texts.

I will accompany each position with a small comment.

And you will carefully study them, and also think about how many cruel murders are on your conscience ...

METHOD #1 - Make a banal and flimsy header.

This is the easiest way to kill. If you make a banal headline, then no one wants to read your advertising text further.

And they will tell you - "What a boring author wrote?"

Since then generally to write further? It will be wasted time. Therefore, then the advertising text is easier to kill immediately. Have not had time to start a romantic relationship with him ...

METHOD #2 - Forget about subtitles.

The task of the subtitles is to be companions of the reader throughout the text. Subheads help to structure the text and keep the reader's attention clearly.

Moreover, it will be convenient for your audience to get acquainted with such text. If you want to break such a reader's idyll, kill the subtitles, and then the text will lose its "guides".

And without guides, it is difficult to find the light at the end of the tunnel or to go out on at least some path in a dark, dense forest.

METHOD #3 - Do not try to show the benefits of your offer.

The benefits of your proposal is one of the main elements of the text that helps readers evaluate how tempting your offer is for them.

With the help of benefits, you could destroy many doubts.

But why do it if you have an order - to eliminate the advertising text without fanfare.

Thoughts killer: there are benefits - there is a problem; no benefits - no problem.

And remember - a unique selling proposition needs to be destroyed immediately, otherwise it can lead an army of benefits and give you a retaliatory strike.

METHOD #4 - Make up some feedback.

Why communicate with direct customers (if they already exist at all) when you can come up with reviews yourself, paint everything in epistolary perfection and bring yourself to a creative orgasm?

Want to kill your text? So do it. Compose tales from which Uncle G. Kh. Anderson would have covered himself and washed his own waterfall of tears ...

METHOD #5 - Specially forget about guarantees

Buyers are interested in warranty. They worry that their so hard earned money can be wasted.

After all, if you sweetly "promise" them frank bullshit, then after tasting they will want to throw out all their anger at someone.

But ... As soon as they see that your text has no guarantees - FIG you, not money! You can immediately send your text to the scaffold ...

METHOD #6 – Do not try to ask questions and answer them.

The question is one of the tools to attract the attention of the reader and hold it.

We ask the question to which the reader wants to get an answer - he is with us for a few more moments.

If you do not use this classic technique - "zvizdets" your advertising text.

Readers are becoming uninteresting - and they will find a more exciting alternative.

METHOD #7 - just speak and not prove

Evidence helps win readers trust.

The author does not just talk about an excellentopportunity but provides concrete evidence. Readers believe him. And that's good.

What is good for the author is bad for the killer. Without evidence, your advertising text will suffocate like a man without air.

METHOD #8 - no need to respect the readers.

Write in a frankly selfish style, tell only about yourself. Why should a text killer think about readers?

He focused his attention on the victim. Want to kill the text? Speak to your readers in a "familiar manner" as if you were sitting on a bench with a beer in your hands, flipping the rotten seeds that were accidentally found in a pocket full of holes.

Use harsh words as well as yard slang. You can do it - and the thing is in the hat.

METHOD #9 - write long sentences and use large paragraphs.

For a text killer, there is nothing better than an irritated reader ... A professional text killer will not miss another opportunity to annoy a reader.

To do this, it is enough to use bulky paragraphs and long sentences so that the reader loses the idea before he has time to learn it.

METHOD #10 – make mistakes in every word.

The more errors in your text - so it looks more like the main mistake of nature.

METHOD #11 - no free test versions.

If you offer to buy cool software worth $ 1000 and do not provide buyers with a free opportunity to test it - instead of sales figures, you will receive a kingdom of donut holes.

So the reader will think that you are "blowing it up", like a thin ball and you want to launch it on an airy erotic journey ... Yeah, right! Three-two-one - "BOOM!"

METHOD #12 - too small or saturated font.

Imagine a reader who needs to touch the screen with his eyelashes to read your text?

Or maybe it is better for him to move 20 meters away from the computer and check his vision, as in the office of an oculist?

Better yet, choose the smallest font and immediately sell a magnifying glass to readers at the price of an exclusive Porsche.

Win-win option!

It is better to immediately put a bullet in the forehead of your text. Or the reader himself will do it for you, in any case - the lethal outcome ...

METHOD #13 - enter "order now" every 20 words.

The more magical red button "order now" in your text - the more chances to scare off buyers.

Therefore, put this button over the text as many times as possible ...

Only then you have to press a completely different "red button" that will erase your text even from the memories ...

METHOD #14 - there are no comparisons with competitors at all, or there is a direct comparison with competitors.

The ability to delicately distinguish one's offer from competitors, without naming a single name or offending anyone, is talent.

But killers have their talent.

Here you can make a choice: either not at all to compare with similar products - let the reader do it himself, or frankly destroy the competitors with a word.

Where it leads? In addition, in the final account, your text will be destroyed, not the products of competitors ...

METHOD #15 - do not try to talk about yourself.

The reader, before clicking on your magic red button "order now", should clearly understand who you are.

If you are an unknown person who has not achieved anything himself - what can you teach or can you sell something useful?

The obvious suspicion is "in front of me another Internet fraudster, issuing Mr. ... for candy."

The more the reader learns about you and your company, the more he will believe you (if, of course, there is something to believe...)

On the other hand, the killers sneeze on it. Why does my text need this? The verdict is no life sentence, death sentence, period.

METHOD #16 - do not place accents.

The text - the victim of the upcoming murder - should not have accents (underlines, highlighting, highlighting, etc.)

Everything should look like a solid mess of letters and words ... Then the last word should not be spoken, because they will not be noticed anyway and will immediately be given a lethal injection.

METHOD #17 - forget about something for free, everything should be paid.

Text killer will NEVER offer anything for free. What for? Everyone wants everything on the ball, and you need to shell out.

And it does not matter that the "free marshmallow" still attracts everyone because it increases the effect of the cost of the whole product.

Although, what's the point of talking about it to the killer, if his business is just to pull the trigger ...

METHOD #18- very small or very expensive price.

No matter how much you praise your advertised product, the reader will form an opinion about whether it was worth it ...

When I see trainings of some specialists who are not interested in $ 1000, I find it funny and sad for those who pay money for it.

On the other hand, what really useful can be learned at the training for $ 10?

If you want to kill your text - shock the price, and it will play its role even better than the 5-time Oscar winner.

Part 5. 99 MARKETING IDEAS

FOR COPYWRITING

Every day you increasingly hear from different people the maxims that a copywriter must be a good marketer.

That's just not all writing people understand the intricacies of marketing. And not all the details need a copywriter.

Today I have prepared 99 marketing ideas for copywriters for you. We will talk about this very marketing in relation to copywriting.

You will not absorb the grueling theoretical pairs but enjoy the clear, structured and really sensible aroma..

99 marketing ideas that most direct related to the copywriting market.

Idea #1- regardless of whether the title is text or

book title - your message should be persuasive, and just

is obliged to form the desire of readers to learn the details.

Idea #2 - Did you notice that the most effective headlines always report

news or focused solely on the interests of the target audience?

Idea #3 - your readers need benefits and benefits, not standard statements and cliches.

Idea #4 - do not limit yourself to describing some of the benefits of your product; be sure to tell readers what they will lose if they don't get it.

Idea #5 - if you wish to draw the reader's attention to an important idea - it should be reflected in the text at least 3 times in different formats.

Idea #6 is an old saying "The more you say, the more you sell" is true: a long text is more convincing than a short one.

Idea #7 - if you want to find a good copywriter - first you need to find a "hungry" reader and consumer - this will help give your ad a more saturated color.

Idea #8 - a good copywriter never works from 9.00 to 17.00 - he always has a pencil and a notebook with him, so that he can write down a successful thought in time and not lose it on the way home.

 Idea #9 - your headline should appeal to a specific target audience if you learn the details about your potential customers in advance - you will immediately save yourself from many unnecessary marketing activities.

Idea #10 - put in the header the most important benefit, so that the reader instantly gets an answer to his question "So what is interesting for me here?"

Idea #11 - regardless of the fact that curiosity has always been a powerful emotion to attract attention - do not flirt with it in the text, it is better to immediately inform readers about the specific benefits.

Idea #12 - news is a great way to attract attention in the headline, so when you have news, shout it out loud and clear.

Idea #13 - put "Simple and Fast" in the message headers - just make sure that this is actually the case.

Idea #14 - your text should be made as if you are communicating with a friend - be friendly and show your individuality in writing.

Idea #15 - add enthusiasm and passion to your texts - sometimes it seems superfluous, but in fact fascinates readers.

Idea #16 - write for your ideal reader and use personalized "You" and "Yours". Even if thousands of people read your texts, anyway, each of them will feel the personal appeal.

Idea #17 - in order not to lose readers in the middle of the text, always end the page with an incomplete sentence - the first part on one page, and the sequel - on another.

Idea #18 - your texts will be read easily if you use spaces between paragraphs, and one paragraph should not exceed 5-6 lines.

Idea #19 - to simplify the reading of your texts, use and highlight the necessary key thoughts so that the reader will get to know them.

Idea #20 - There should be some convincing subheadings in your text that will help keep the reader's attention throughout the text.

Idea #21 - your subheadings should contain a separate "selling" message - then readers who simply "scan" your texts will definitely pay attention to them.

Idea #22 - use graphic tricks to draw attention to your message and make it easier to learn - bullets, numbers, capital letters, underlines, italics, frames, etc.

Idea #23 - effective copywriters always recognize the greatest pain of their readers, focus their conviction around this pain, and then offer a solution on how to eliminate such pain.

Idea #24- You should think of your "P.S." as a second heading. This is the second most readable part of the text, so strengthen it in some way.

Idea #25 - in fact, your readers are on the verge of buying what they don't yet know. If you charge your texts with powerful guarantees - they are able to dispel existing doubts and take the necessary action.

Idea #26 - pay due attention to the drawing up of guarantees, because this is another selling opportunity, make your guarantee unique, and at the same time probable and possible.

Idea #27 - several guarantees are much better than one guarantee.

Idea #28 - there are obvious benefits that you must note in your texts, and in many cases hidden guarantees have a more convincing effect - remember this.

Idea #29 - readers buy based on emotions, not logic. 5 key emotions on the way to the sale - love, greed, pride, fear and guilt. Be guided by these emotions, and your copywriting will become more effective.

Idea #30 - you have to believe in what you sell. If readers do not feel this in the text - they will not read it to the end.

Idea #31 - compose your texts in such a way that a 5th grader can read them easily, because approximately 30% of the audience cannot read above this level. If you want readers to fully understand you - be easier.

Idea #32 - copywriters should put graphic images in their texts that will be convince readers. Their task is not to decorate the text, but to involve the audience in it.

Idea #33 - the words you use and combine will influence your sales figures, so carefully come to the selection of words, not empty words ...

Idea #34 - most direct sales are done between 3rd and 7th contact. Therefore, if you want to make a sale using one text - you must sell the benefits about 7 times.

Idea #35 - be neat and sophisticated when using 7 selling items. They can be placed in the headline, subheadings, "bullet", reviews, guarantees, history, postscript, etc.

Idea #36 - postscript is a great opportunity to add another benefit to the text and enhance the overall selling effect.

Idea #37 - To make postscript more visible - select it with a separate font, size, underlines, and other graphic elements.

Idea #38 - people remember the very first and last thing they see or hear. Therefore, use your key points of persuasion at the beginning and end of your writing.

Idea #39 - All successful texts contain a call to action, so do not forget about this element.

Idea #40 - your call to action is not worth a penny, if you are not clear with your readers - tell them what you want from them, exactly how, when, and give them an incentive to do it.

Idea #41 - a successful call to action includes a summary of the offer, the cost of the product, an increase in its value (for example, with the help of discounts), additional offers and bonuses.

Idea #42 - if your reader puts the text aside to study it later - consider that you have lost a client. Therefore, you need to compose your texts in such a way that readers want to read them now.

Idea #43 it a good way to force the reader to take the desired action - inform him about the limited validity of the offer: price increases after a certain period, the disappearance of discounts or special bonuses for the first 100 buyers.

Idea #44 - additional incentives to take action include: secret bonuses, limited offers, fears of losing bonuses.

Idea #45 - as long as you write convincingly in your text - the target reader carefully follows the entire text, if it is not targeted - even a short advertising message will not arouse his interest.

Idea #46 - advertising texts are better read when they are in the form of an article. This is a great way to tell the reader that he can acquire what is being told.

Idea #47 - since fear is the strongest emotion - most people make emotional purchases if you use warnings about the fear of loss in your writing.

Idea #48 – It's challenging to win and keep the attention of the reader throughout the text. If you give your writing a bit of drama, it will help keep the reader on your pages.

Idea #49 – using rage, anger and resentment at some problems that can solve your product, you have the opportunity to attract and hold the attention of readers.

Idea #50 - the client always responds to your talent as a copywriter, not to criticism from colleagues or competitors.

Idea #51 - when writing texts, do not hesitate to use verbs and adjectives - they allow you to draw the desired picture in the imagination of readers. Your audience will be happy to read the text and absorb every thought.

Idea #52 - after the readers have finished studying your text, they should get the impression that they felt, held in their hands, looked, sniffed and tasted your product.

Idea #53 - your text is an extremely important tool for those who want to learn more about your product, so make the most of this desire to convince the reader to buy this product.

Idea #54 - to write an effective text, you need to make it "hot." Therefore, it is advisable to start writing the text not from the very beginning, but already from the middle to the end, and then - to think separately about the beginning.

Idea #55 is another way to start a text - just write everything that comes to mind related to the product, after which these records are systematized, corrected and give them a logical look.

Idea #56 - imagine that you write your text personally for a friend - tell him all the good things about your product.

Idea #57 - the first sentence of your text (whether it is a story, a shocking message, a news story, an announcement or a story), should continue the thought set forth in the heading.

Idea #58 - the only style that works for all types of copywriting is an imitation of the manufacturer's communication with the client.

Idea #59 - Actual copywriting works better because it informs readers of a large number of facts that dispel all doubts.

Idea #60 - do not leave your best benefit for last. Indicate the strengths immediately in the first paragraph, or they may remain unread.

Idea #61 - your headline should do more than just attract the attention of readers. It should attract the attention of readers who are the immediate target audience of the text.

Idea #62 - there are many ways to activate the creativity of your presentation, for a start - you just need to free the brain from unnecessary thoughts and in a quiet environment to concentrate fully on the text.

Idea #63 is best done using a computer's text editor to help you quickly write and edit.

Idea #64 is the best way to feel your audience - to study the demographic and psychological characteristics of your potential customers.

Idea #65 - you should regularly test regular updates of your texts in order to keep them successful all the time.

Idea #66 - find a way to convince the reader that the proposed ordering and payment method is actually very beneficial for him.

Idea #67 - explain what exactly your guarantees are better than the guarantees of other sellers - this will help you remove fear from buyers before purchasing an unknown product.

Idea #68 - a limited sentence will increase the response of your text - try to find a way to use this approach to encourage readers to quickly take the desired action.

Idea #69 - your reader may not understand your thoughts if you use highly professional slang, so be simple.

Idea #70 - everyone wants to know that something is interesting for him in his text - therefore, use the list of specific benefits.

Idea #71 - if you have a large customer base, include specific data in your text. Then new customers will feel as if they are joining a large number of like-minded people, and they will understand that they can lose a lot if they do not join.

Idea #72 - try to read your text without headings and subtitles, if it doesn't sell - rewrite it or strengthen it.

Idea #73 – If you are having difficulty identifying the specific benefits of a product - talk to the manufacturer, seller, or consultant - they will help you to feel the full value of the offer.

Idea #74 - if your product or service is new, explain what is new and why it's so great. In this case, do not even think about talking about "novelty", if in fact, it is far from the truth.

Idea #75 - if your product is designed for an audience belonging to a single gender, be sure to include in the text the idea that this product could be an excellent gift.

Idea #76 - if your company has extensive experience in the market - feel free to talk about it. Your customers want to know if you can guarantee them good service for many years.

Idea #77 - Walk around the room and read your text out loud.

If you breathed the air somewhere in the middle of a sentence, think how to make it shorter or split it into several parts.

Idea #78 - tell readers why they have a certain education, income level, special interests. And then explain that you address them precisely because of this specialization. This will help readers to take your offer more seriously.

Idea #79 - when listing all the benefits of your product, make sure that you name the most important benefits, because some of them may not be so obvious to your readers.

Idea #80 - when you address your text to educated and culturally enlightened people, try to create some kind of tradition.

Idea #81 - everyone likes to feel elected and invited, so instead of "buy" use "fill up the collection", "increase", "strengthen" and other approximate expressions.

Idea #82 - never contact the reader "dear customer" if he is not your customer - it will only annoy.

Idea #83 - during a greeting, identify your readers by name or interest, the use of "lady and gentleman" turnovers only reduces efficiency.

Idea #84 - if your product has been subjected to some kind of research - do not forget to report it in the text. This will increase the weight of your product in the eyes of the reader.

Idea #85 - if your company is a small structural element of a larger and well-known company - report it, because with this step you increase the degree of trust.

Idea #86 - Does your text contain information about how the customer should use your product or service? This will help the reader to associate himself with this product.

Idea #87 - if your product has special technical features and differences - explain it in a simple, clear language.

Idea #88 - if your total product includes any accessories, manuals, or additional "gadgets" that will help potential buyers save time and money - report it.

Idea #89 - when you send a new offer to your customers, be sure to thank them for their previous cooperation with your company.

Idea #90 - small texts are more effective if you are not aiming to force the reader to buy something right now, in this case, it is better to use long texts.

Idea #91 - if with the help of a long text you wish to stimulate the reader to make a purchase instantly - you should give him a large list of benefits in order to crush all his doubts.

Idea #92 - always explain to your readers the reason why they should perform the action. Causes is a collection of the benefits they will receive from this action.

Idea #93 - you will inspire confidence if you tell about the quality and service when buying your product.

Idea #94 - do not get carried away by the strict official style in your letters, it is more suitable for press releases.

Idea #95 - the same words have different meanings for representatives of different categories of readers. Make sure you use the right words for your target audience.

Idea #96 - let your readers understand why it is profitable for them to buy the product using the method you suggested, and not by any other.

Idea #97 - your postscript should reinforce the selling effect of the entire text and convince those readers who have learned it fluently.

Idea #98 - use conflicting and controversial thoughts in the headlines - they increase interest in the text.

Idea #99 - Curiosity is a powerful copywriting tool. If a person is curious, it is difficult for him to keep from reading your text. Use this feature in headings and subheadings to make reading more fun.

Part 6. COMMERCIAL

SUGGESTION

The most common type of selling texts are commercial offers.

Let's start the conversation with why we need commercial offers at all and how we use them in the company.

The classic option is when the manager speaks with the client on the phone.

The client may be tired of listening to the bleating of a weak sales manager or your offer is not interesting to him, and he, in order to get rid, says: "Well, send a commercial one".

The sales manager is happy - he believes that this is already a success since such an interest has been shown.

In fact, of course, there is not much interest, but there is an agreement to send a commercial offer, and this is an occasion to catch on, write and send an offer, and then call the company and use it as a reason for a new contact.

The following situation, when the client is really interested in what you offer.

But it is difficult for him to perceive a lot of information by ear, he wants to visualize what you are telling him, and he also says: send commercial.

That is, in case of cold sales with the help of phone calls, the commercial offer is quite an active tool for work.

The next aspect of the application of commercial offers is cold mailing.

When we send out mailings to customers in order to generate some incoming calls, initiate interest in the product, we do it on the so-called cold base.

This is not a spam mailing when we indiscriminately have a suggestion about machine tools for laundry and hairdressing.

These are potential customers who once in some way dealt with our company, but did not become current customers - they did not buy anything from us. Either we intersected with them somewhere at the exhibition, took a business card at the conference from someone, or they left contacts on our website.

That is, these are people who, in principle, our product may be interesting, but so far they either don't know about our company, either don't remember or don't think.

We send out commercial offers to them, and some of these customers are beginning to be interested, to call, to find out, to order.

Or, after the mailing, we ourselves call the telephone calls and use the fact of sending the letter as a reason to call and start a conversation.

Another option for the application of a commercial offer is the announcement of new product positions.

If you enter a new position in the product range, you have developed a new product or service and want to inform potential or current customers about it; you also do this by sending commercial offers.

In addition to potential and existing customers, there is also such a category as the former.

And the task of returning former customers and making them operational again is very important, especially in a downturn in the market.

We write letters to them asking them to return, but we can also send them just a commercial offer and tell them about a new product or new promotions.

Sooner or later they will be interested in something; some proposal will seem important to them. And they will start buying from us again.

If we carry out any promotions, discounts, sales, give customers bonuses for certain purchases, we also use commercial offers as a tool to convey this information to customers.

There is another interesting point: commercial offers can be used to poison the lives of competitors, and sometimes to intercept their customers.

For example, there is a company X on the market to which you want to supply something, but it is not buying from you but from your competitor Peter. And this Peter has been supplying them for many years what you want to deliver to this company yourself.

What are you doing? You start monthly, for example, send your business offers to firm X.

You understand that neither from this commercial offer nor from the next one, probably, the sale will not take place.

But each such commercial proposal undermines Peter's position in relation to this company, because, naturally, you try to offer conditions better than Peter suggests, because you want to intercept a client, and you are ready to give a good discount to attract him.

What does company X do? She immediately forwards this offer to Peter with the words: "Peter, look, and here they are offering such prices. Maybe you too will move in the price? "And sooner or later, Peter will either have to move or give up his position.

That is a pressure tool. And Peter is also not iron; Peter can make a mistake: put it wrong or not, let down his buyer. If Peter made a mistake, this is a reason for firm X to look for another supplier.

And the first, whom Firm X will remember, will be you, because you regularly touch it with your commercial offers, regularly remind yourself, make it clear that "I am in reserve while you work with Peter, but if anything, I am here." When such a situation comes, the company will remember you.

This is not all ways, but these are the main points.

We are now talking about cold commercial offers, that is, when the client either does not know about you or else he does not buy from you.

There are also hot commercial offers when the client is ready to buy, a deal for an ointment, only here are some formalities to be sent in the form of a commercial offer and settlement, but we are not talking about it now.

We are talking about how to increase sales with the help of cold commercial offers.

Why do we need to actively send cold commercial offers?

Naturally, to increase our sales funnel.

For example, we have a cold sales department that makes calls.

How many calls does the sales manager average per day? If he makes 50 quality calls to customers per day, that's great. Because on average, not very smart managers make much less - 5-10 calls, or even sit and wait for incoming calls.

But even if each manager will make 50 outgoing calls, you can send commercial offers at times, tens of thousands of times more. If you have a normal, proven base, if it is regularly replenished, then, making such mailings, you significantly increase the sales funnel, and accordingly, improve the result.

Well, then we need to talk about the quality of these proposals because we have already discussed that quality increases conversion.

Hooked on more customers — involved in reading — interested in the offer — sold out.

So what to do to hook the client with our Commercial Offer?

Let's start with the most common mistakes.

Error one: incorrectly identified customer needs.

Since commercial offers that sell texts that we send to customers are part of the sales system, the same laws apply as in direct sales.

If you have not identified customer needs or identified them incorrectly, the sale will not take place; or you will meet a large number of objections, or just get rejected. That is, your task is to send commercial offers to customers, either to find out in advance their needs for a preliminary telephone conversation, or, if it is not possible to conduct such a conversation, calculate, collect information, collect a file on the client.

Then you can talk to him in the text about his needs in his area of interest.

The next mistake is that the commercial offer was sent to a representative of the target audience.

You must understand to whom you are sending a commercial offer. If this is a person who does not take decisions, or a person to whom this product is not at all interesting, of course, commercial proposals will fly into the basket.

And analyze the internal errors that are contained in the process of directly writing the text.

The most key mistake is the text "mumbles". They begin with the words: "We are a wonderful company, we have been on the market for 20 years, we are leaders there in a certain industry, winners of numerous exhibitions ..."

This is all uninteresting! A person does not want to read about how cool you are; a person wants to become cool himself.

If you help, explain to him how he can become great with your help, then he will read your offer and will react to it.

And if there is another 99th letter that begins with the words "we, we, we", as a rule, all this causes boredom and irritation.

The next commercial offer error is an abstraction.

No specific offer. Very often there are letters in which they offer to buy what is impossible to buy: it is impossible to buy cooperation, partnership.

You can buy a product or a specific service. "The firm" SEO Profi "offers cooperation."

The company "SEO Profi" think: well, it is clear from the name, what we do. In fact, not everyone understands.

We must offer to buy, order a specific service.

And it is desirable to offer one service in one offer, and not to try to throw the entire profile of the company into one letter so that we understand.

Classic example

"Event Market" offers:

• weddings;

• funeral arrangements;

• corporate parties;

• excursions around the city;

• hang-gliding.

You do not know whether to order a wedding first, then fly a hang glider and a funeral right away?

Or what? What do they want from us? The client does not respond to such offers.

That is, the client's attention is extremely dispersed. You have to understand that any decision maker receives a huge amount of information every day, and he will not react to the situation when you need to think, understand, find out and delve into a long list of what is being offered.

Such commercial offers come to me in bundles, in which everything that the firm offers is simply stupidly listed.

That is, the sender thinks that he is sending the client's last offer to the client for the last time and you have to push everything in there.

I will not read this - I have no time.

Another mistake: send the same commercial offer to all clients, all groups of clients.

For each such group, for each situation, for each product, there should be a separate commercial offer made up for this client, for his specific needs.

Single templates do not work. Firstly, the client immediately sees that this is a sample commercial offer, in which you just changed the data and sent it to everyone else, and secondly, if you didn't guess the needs, and we already talked about it, the client will not respond. This is not a letter about him, and he will not read it.

Therefore, for each client, we write an individual version of the Commercial Offer.

When we write a commercial offer, we must clearly set ourselves a goal: what we want the client to do in the end.

Maybe our goal is to sell a product. But this is not the only goal.

Sometimes the purpose of a commercial offer is for the client to simply call, come to the office, respond to the letter, request a catalog, pay the bill - that is, each specific commercial offer must have its own clear purpose for which it is written. And the simpler the goal, the higher the conversion. Because selling plastic windows, for example, with the help of a commercial offer is much more difficult than making a customer call and order a free metering.

And you can sell windows at the stage of measurement.

Commercial offers are a network of hooks.

We have already talked about the scattered attention of managers, which is constantly disconnected and closed from external incoming information.

Our task is to build a commercial offer as a whole network of hooks or bridges, which leads the client by the hand through our entire letter to our key point, where it says "buy, pay, transfer money".

We have no margin for error.

Understanding how many problems a person solves today in the modern world, we need to know that he has switched to another browser window - and forgot about us.

That is, any of our mistakes in the text are, as with sappers, it deprives our commercial proposal of a chance for a result.

Because if the client left him, he would not return to him.

What should be the structure of the commercial offer, so that it has the effect?

First, we need a headline.

The most common title in commercial offers is "Commercial Offer".

That is, you are writing to a person who still does not know about you or the product, that this is a commercial offer, and the person immediately understands that it will now be a matter of buying some product.

Your task is to intrigue the client, catch on some kind of hook, make it read further.

We talked about the hook network: the purpose of the heading is to make the first paragraph read. Do not buy, do not read the whole letter, but at least make you read the first paragraph.

And in the first paragraph, you put the next hook, which should make him read the next one.

And so on. Thus, when you construct it, there will be a chance to bring the person to the end of the letter.

The headline is what almost 100% of the recipients of the letter read.

When the addressee receives your letter, he decides whether to read or not.

And, when evaluating, people look first at the headline in order to understand what it is all about.

Therefore, if you have a catchy headline, says something that is important to the client, he will read further, at least the first paragraph.

If the heading is boring or nothing, or it's not at all clear what will be discussed, the client will not waste his time.

Thus, there is a very hard screening - what to read, what not to read.

Head time is always limited.

Next, we need to talk about the dragon, that is, to identify the problem of the client.

I call this "point to disease".

We know where the client "hurts", and before proposing a solution, we press on the sore spot so that the pain intensifies and the desire to heal is strengthened with it.

After that, we need to inform the client that we have a cure - a magic pill, supermaze, etc.

We have already attracted the attention of the client to ourselves, having talked about his problems, so now he calmly perceives the offer of a solution in the form of a product.

6.1. FORMULA OF WRITING OF HEADING

I would like to once again emphasize the importance of the title for the selling text.

Everyone knows that.

Everyone also knows how difficult it is to find a good title for a particular occasion.

We are always tormented by doubts about the appropriateness of a particular reception.

We can like it, but how will the direct target audience perceive it?

By and large, all the techniques, techniques and formulas are good - when they looked appropriate and executed sensibly.

I want to share with you a unique heading formula that even our grandchildren can survive.

Changing tastes, goals, decision criteria, and the power of this title will never change.

This is already a well-known formula, which is indicated by all copywriting experts, but for its final effect some procedures should be carried out, and then everything will be type-top.

As far as you remember, a good headline:

• immediately identifies the target audience • intrigues • communicates the benefits • speaks the truth

Consequently, our universal formula must take into account all 4 criteria identified.

Immediately strike out one of them - the default title should tell the reader the truth.

It makes no sense to be misleading from the first lines - this has a bad effect on sales figures.

Next - intrigue is easily solved by creating a header in an interrogative form.

If we ask an apt question, on a subconscious level, I want to know the answer to it.

And when we conduct a preliminary study, which questions are most often asked by representatives of our target audience, the search is greatly simplified.

Now I tell you the backbone of our formula:

"How (desired action or desired result)?"

The element of the "how" formula and interrogative strategy is already an intrigue.

The element of the formula "(the desired action or the desired result)" is intended to designate the target audience. Moreover, the trick is that here it is not even necessary to directly indicate the target audience.

That is, no need to say - a woman, a man, a mechanic, an adult, etc.

The very formulation of the desired action and result immediately reflects the preferences and needs of a specific target audience.

For example:

1. "learn to play the harmonica" - anyone who wants to master the game of this musical instrument

2. "pass the driving test" - likewise, we have before us any potential driver who is going to take the driving test

3. "meet a girl" - here without comments

4. "to issue a price list" - any entrepreneur who has the task of developing an effective price list.

And we get the backbone of the title, for example: "How to get acquainted with the girl?".

The benefit of this simple formula is that it will easily take root on the Internet since almost any correctly chosen formulation will correspond to the search query of the desired target audience.

It seems like all is well. The formula is already simple, and many people set it up as an example. They even call it "how to formula".

But my personal opinion - all this is not enough. For the simple reason - there is not one of the key characteristics of an effective headline, which we talked about earlier.

Namely - there is no message about the benefits.

For example, what is the benefit of saying a simple headline "How to meet a girl"?

There is no direct indication, and the reader has to think out.

Therefore, I propose a classical formula to significantly strengthen and present it in the following form:

"Like (desired action or desired result) + AMP"

The task of the amplifier is to communicate the direct benefit of immersion in the text.

The second task is to select exactly our text against the background of similar ones.

Imagine how you enter into the search box the query "How to sell an apartment."

Before you open the issue tape, and in it, you see the headers, let's say:

1. "How to sell an apartment?"

2. "How to sell an apartment more expensive than its market value?"

One can argue for a very long time about the clumsiness and verbal clutter of the second option, but one has only to wear the skin of a person who enters such a request, and the opinion about the second heading is changing.

When we look at the first option, and then at the second - it seems to us that the first option is filled with general advice, and the second is already more specific and attractive in terms of its information value.

But then just a little clarification - do not forget about the characteristic "to inform the truth."

I just do not want the title to be really translated into the text, and the information itself did not meet the expectations.

Therefore, when preparing the text itself, it is necessary to initially deviate from the manner of presenting general information, justifying it with the boring phrase "for someone this information will be valuable."

Selling text should not be guided by "someone" ...

On the contrary, the more representatives of the real target audience he collects, the better for sales.

You can also ask me - what to sell in such a heading if it is inherently not selling, but purely informational?

In this and all the sweetness of the juice - with a similar title, we move away from the effect of frontal pairing.

We do not offer a service, but information. This is done to warm up to the service itself - cooperation with a realtor on the sale of an apartment.

But let's go back to the goal of writing the title, continue the dive.

What can act as an amplifier? There are a lot of answers here, depending on the scope of activities and the specifics of the service, as well as the psychological subtleties of the target audience.

But for academic character I will give a few classic "amplifiers", accompanied by their example:

1. Speed - "How to apply for a visa to Canada in 3 days?"

2. The specific amount - "How to make money on copywriting the first $ 1000?"

3. Comparison - "How to keep an Instagram account, like a rock star?"

4. Simplification - "How to choose a gift to the boss without visiting the store?"

5. Contrast - "How to make fondue, if cooking is alien to you?"

6. Collection of options - "How to tie a tie in ten fashionable ways?"

7. Independent work - "How to promote a blog without outside help?"

8. Savings - "How to buy plane tickets, saving at least 20%?"

9. The combination of amplifiers - "How to earn the first $ 1000 in copywriting in 7 days?"

By the way, for the beauty and the best persuasiveness, it is not always necessary to observe the exact sequence of the elements of the formula.

I hope you get the gist of my reasoning, and now everything seems simple and clear to you.

6.2. OFFER

Just offering a product is not enough. After all, we are not the only ones on the market. And the fact that we have a product and we want to sell it is our problem.

It does not make sense the letter that tells just about what you want. And the fact that you have some kind of candy is also not interesting to read.

Tell me what I'll get besides candy if I buy it from you. Because not only you have candy, but also Nicholas and Peter. And Patrick has candy twice as much as you, and the price is the same. Therefore, in order for me to buy exactly your candy, you have to perform something, dance, promise and give it to me.

It will be about marketing efforts that you are ready to undertake to get me as a client.

Customers know their value. Clients understand that they are a tasty morsel for you, and are ready, like a pretty girl, to see with interest how you will fight other applicants in order to give yourself to the strongest.

Or sell with the greatest profit.

The most important thing here is not to overdo it in order not to get into bondage to the client at all, but if you do not make efforts in this direction, you will fail. Especially in the conditions of a permanent crisis, a drop in purchasing power: a crisis in our economy is a phenomenon that is regularly returning, so if at the moment when you are reading a book, the economy suddenly grows - be sure that soon it will start falling again.

You told the client that you have a cool product, about how cool you are, what you need to buy from you.

So what? Why should a customer break down and start buying? Therefore, you need to make an increase in our offer.

And the technique that allows you to make this gain is called an "offer".

You have a certain product, and your competitors also have such a product, and the prices are about the same, it is unlikely that someone in the market has a unique product and there are no competitors.

The competition is high; there are many offers, it is necessary to stand out for something.

You must clearly answer the client to the question: what will I receive if I respond to the letter if I respond to the commercial offer?

Offer is your unique selling proposition.

What can be the unique trade offer today?

It is unlikely that you will be able to offer some kind of super goods that others do not have.

But you can offer terms of delivery, which others do not have, some kind of discount, which others do not have at the moment, any additional options.

This will be your unique selling proposition. To understand how the offer works, consider this example.

Imagine that you went to the market to buy tomatoes. And in front of you are long rows of goods and a series of sellers. And each has a complete set of juicy and fragrant tomatoes. All tidy, even and neat. And probably from the same supplier - from the same vegetable base.

And the price of all the sellers for them is about the same. Sellers have long agreed among themselves and do not fight at prices.

You walk, touch, smell, ask the price and don't understand who you should buy from. Suddenly one salesman grabs you by the hand and speaks with a characteristic accent:

"Dear, take two kilograms of tomatoes from me, then I will give you a jar of strawberries as a gift."

And now an occasion to think.

His neighbor on the counter smiles as broadly as he is also happy to give you two kilograms of tomatoes but does not offer anything else. A can of strawberries is so great.

Children will be happy. And no need to spend money.

This favorably distinguishes this proposal from the general range and makes you wonder. This is the extra benefit. This is a Unique Trading Offer.

They may be an additional discount, special price. But it is better if it is a bonus, an additional gift, special terms of delivery or payment, the opportunity to receive something else - status.

For example: "Our store opens next Monday. Come to us! "What is the incentive to come to the store on Monday? Just because it opens? Few shops open up.

And here: "Our store opens next Monday. Anyone who makes a purchase on Monday at our store has a coupon for a $ 50 discount as a gift! "- this is a real incentive to come, this is already an offer, this is already some kind of unique offer.

If the price plays a role for you and discounts are important to you, it makes sense to come to the store on Monday because the very fact of opening a store is not a reason for this.

The same thing: "Open your brokerage account with us and start making money on the exchange".

All companies that offer to open a brokerage account, lure customers.

But: "Open your brokerage account with us - and we will give you a personal investment advisor for a month for free" - this is a unique selling proposition.

Because the cost of a brokerage account is about the same for everyone, someone is a bit more expensive; someone is a bit cheaper.

But there is an incentive to go and open; there is an incentive to take some action.

That is, the offer formula - perform the action that I need, and get something beneficial.

If you have such an offer, you look favorably against the background of all other commercial proposals that the decision maker received on the same day.

If not, then it is not clear why he should read your letter and generally react to it.

Or, "With my help, I propose to learn how to write high-conversion texts that will double your income from sending commercial offers." All offer.

And here, for example: "Buy a ticket to my seminar and get a free audit of your commercial offer!" Is an offer.

When you offer something, let's get something on top. This will be your offer.

6.3. DEADLINE

The next important element that we have to introduce in our commercial proposals is called "deadline".

We convinced the client that we have a cool product, we convinced that you need to buy from us.

The next challenge that your business proposals must solve is to explain to the customer what to buy right now.

People tend to put things off for later. "I'll think about it tomorrow."

They receive your offer, see an interestingoffer, say to themselves: "Super. It will be necessary for these guys to buy their products. Interesting terms and conditions offer "- and put your letter aside, because someone just wrote them a personal message on Skype, or you need to urgently read someone's Facebook post, or it's time to go for dinner, etc.

The chances that after lunch or after reading the 18 posts in the friendly client the client will return to your letter are insignificant.

Because you are not alone with him, and more recent letters will fall on top of this pile, and there is not a lot of space in his head for storing such information. And there are always better things to do.

He must, without closing your letter, reach for his wallet and perform some targeted action.

If the client postpones the decision to purchase - it is likely that he will postpone it forever.

Therefore, we need to create a tight time limit so that the client understands that if he does not do what we need right now, he will miss some important benefit. And so we need a deadline.

The word English, like other marketing terms. Dead is "dead", line is "line".

In our case, this is the line where special offers die.

That is, for example, you offer some kind of bonus to the client, but it is only valid for 24 hours, and then turns into a pumpkin, like a Cinderella carriage.

What is the deadline in our history with the market and the purchase of tomatoes? You go along the rows, choose tomatoes, and, as we remember, one of the vendors grabs you by the hand and promises a jar of strawberries as a gift if you buy two kilograms of these tomatoes from him.

But you have not reached the end of the series.

You are not sure that there will be any interesting offers or low prices ahead.

You answer the seller: "Wait, brother. Now I'll go to the end of the row; I'll see everything with everyone and then I'll come back to you. "

The seller understands: come. Now you will leave, and it is unlikely that you will return.

Because there, at the end of the row, there are also a couple of good friends with strawberries or strawberries, because you can be too lazy to go back, something can distract you, etc.

The seller understands that it is necessary to forge iron without departing from the cash register.

And then he says: "Take right now, then two cans of strawberries will give."

An example, of course, conditional, to simply illustrate the technique.

But the principle is clear: if you go to look at the tomatoes further, and then still return to this seller, you will receive only one can of strawberries.

The chances that at the end of a row someone else is waiting for you with two banks is a bit.

Is it worth running? We must take on the spot.

This is how the technique called deadline worked.

The seller forced you to decide on the spot, without delay, because before your eyes a substantial benefit from this purchase could evaporate.

And you clung to this opportunity and did not postpone until later.

Our task is to rigidly frame our customers so that they do not throw our letters into indebtedness and endure the trip to our store or order our products indefinitely for tomorrow, but immediately react and reach for the wallet.

Even it is not always necessary to offer a second can of strawberries.

Sometimes it is enough to promise to take away the first one if the client does not take the target action in the appointed time.

As the deadline is formulated in commercial offers and advertising texts:

• "Sale of sheepskin coats with 70% discount. Only until August 15! ";

• "Only this weekend in our restaurant, children eat for free";

• "Pay for the renewal of a subscription to the magazine" Sales Management "until December 31 - and we will leave you the old price".

Deadline is open and closed.

Closed deadline– this is when we clearly mark the date for the client, after which our offer ceases to operate:

• "Only until October 31, you can buy a ticket to a ski resort with a 20% discount";

• "Only on September 1, every tenth visitor of our bar has a pint of beer for free";

• "Only February 14, a discount on rings in our store is 30%".

That is, there is a certain frontier, and it is determined by a calendar day or several days.

There is another kind of closed deadline - goods of the week:

• "The product of the week is a DNX gaming computer mouse. Only this week, it has a special price - $ XXX ";

• "The product of the month - Salamandra boots. Special discount - 18%.

At the same time, pay special attention to the fact that all deadlines must contain exact dates.

Because if you write a "product of the week" on a leaflet, distribute leaflets to potential buyers, they will stay with them for a couple of weeks and then someone will get ready to buy - the discount will not work anymore.

Yes, and a clear date spur better abstract words.

That is when you need to write "this Thursday," be sure to put the exact date in brackets.

When writing about the goods of the week, specify the dates of the beginning and end of the week, etc.

Open deadline – it is such a formulation that does not name a specific date for the termination of special conditions but links it with other factors: availability of seats, availability of goods in a warehouse, number of items sold, etc.

For example: "The first ten customers are a gift" - in my opinion, a weak trigger.

How to understand if you are in the top ten?

Yes, and begin to creep in doubt that, even if you get, they will tell you that you did not hit.

And here is another wording, more feasible: "We sell cars of the last year of release with a 10% discount. There are only ten cars left. "

We are not saying that it will be late tomorrow or next week.

The buyer himself determines when, as it seems to him, he may be late. And, accordingly, it starts to move or not.

"Hurry up! There are only six places left at the David Ogilvy seminar on selling texts. "

If you really want to attend a seminar on selling texts, then the truth will begin to hurry.

After all, six places can sell in one hour. And maybe for three days. Is it worth the risk? It is urgent to make a decision and act.

And you and me open deadline gives excellent opportunities for maneuver.

We can always say that it is for you one more, the last car is in the garage and waiting.

Or that one place to the seminar has not yet been sold, but a lot of applications. Stir.

6.4. CALL TO ACTION

The next important element that I wanted to say is a call to action.

You told the client about the problem, about the product, you explained why you need to buy from you, explained why you need to buy now. Many on this and stop. And forget to explain what to do next. And forget to ask about the purchase.

Explain to the client what to do to make a purchase, and how exactly it should be done. And call to buy.

This should be clearly spelled out, in a prominent place, large. Because the client, as we have said many times, as a child. His attention was scattered, distracted - and that's all, we lost him.

Our task is to take him by the hand and take him to the checkout. Clearly explain to him where to go and what to do.

The action should be simple. There should be no complicated schemes. As soon as some difficulty begins - that's all, our offer is postponed.

• "Buy today a subscription to the magazine" Sales Management "!"

• "Call us - and we will immediately open a brokerage account for you!"

• "Go to the conference site" SALES-2019 "and leave a request!

And then - how to do it.

And here is a common mistake - the conditional form: "If you want to buy a subscription to the magazine, call us on the phone."

No ifs!

By saying "if," you seem to doubt that the customer wants to buy your product. You should not doubt. Then he will not. He wants. He has no other way out. Therefore, always only an affirmative form.

"In order to buy a subscription, call by phone" - in any case not "if".

And yet, one commercial offer - one call to action.

Just like one commercial offer - one goal, one offer, one call to action.

To avoid numerous different ways in which you can get lost and confused.

Clear, simple wording, clear, simple instructions for what to do.

So, summing up the structure of a commercial offer: we attract attention, point to a disease, show a medicine, explain why we need to buy medicine from us, focus attention and explain why we need to buy right now, and urge to buy, explaining how to do it.

Here is such a simple formula.

It works not only in commercial offers but also in advertising texts, in letters, texts on websites, etc.

This formula is universal.

It was not I who invented it, it is described in many books on copywriting, but at the same time it does not lose its effectiveness and, unfortunately, is used very little.

In conclusion, I want to say about one important thing.

In addition to the fact that your sales managers need to know how to make commercial offers, they must also apply this knowledge.

Therefore, it is necessary to introduce such a tool in the company as a checklist for writing commercial offers, with which the manager must consult before he sends his Commercial Proposal: what basic elements should he insert, title, subtitle, offer, etc.

And then you can significantly improve the quality of your commercial proposals and, accordingly, significantly increase the conversion of your selling text.

Part 7. CONCLUSION

In this book, I tried to give as little as possible third-party information. All essentially, how to write the text that sells. I hope that you will use my tips on writing selling texts.

"Our big drawback is that we quickly give up. The surest way to success, all the time trying one more time!" Thomas Edison

 Good luck to you my friend!

I would be grateful for the feedback on the book. Thanks!

I recommend my book "INSTAGRAM MARKETING TIPS"
Secrets of Copywriting for Instagram